ANIMAL WONDERS

Published by Creative Education, Inc., 123 South Broad Street, Mankato, Minnesota
56001

Printed by permission of Wildlife Education, Ltd.

Library of Congress Cataloging-in-Publication Data

Wexo, John Bonnett.
Animal wonders / by John Bonnett Wexo.
p.   cm.
Summary: Describes a wide variety of animal characteristics, including protective
coloration, modes of locomotion, methods of feeding, etc.
ISBN 0-88682-407-9
1. Animals—Miscellanea—Juvenile literature. [1. Animals.] I.Title.
QL49.W485   1991   591—dc20 91-11642 CIP AC

ANIMAL WONDERS

Zoobook Series Created by
John Bonnett Wexo

Written by
John Bonnett Wexo

Zoological Consultant
Charles R. Schroeder, D.V.M.
Director Emeritus
San Diego Zoo &
San Diego Wild Animal Park

Creative Education

Contents

Everything in nature has a purpose. No matter how strange an animal may look to us, there is a reason why it is made the way it is and behaves the way it does. In fact, many of the oddest-looking animals are among the most successful animals on earth. Some of them have strange structures on their bodies to help them get food. Others use peculiar colors and shapes to help them find a mate. And many animals use shapes and colors to keep other animals from fighting with them or eating them.

Like many animals, chameleons (kuh-ME-lee-uns) have a home territory that they defend against all outsiders. The horns of the male Jackson's Chameleon are designed for this purpose. Nobody knows whether the chameleons ever actually use their horns to fight, but they certainly make the animals look like miniature dinosaurs.

The Red Uakari (wah-CAR-ee) uses the color of its face to scare its enemies away. The more angry the monkey gets, the brighter the color becomes. The color is usually enough to chase enemies, so the monkey rarely has to fight.

Shoebill Storks have bills that look like wooden shoes. As strange as they may look to us, these bills are perfect for catching food. The storks use them to scoop up frogs and to dig fish out of the mud.

Harmless animals sometimes look dangerous to keep other animals from eating them. When predators see the huge "teeth" on the head of an Alligator Bug, they often decide that it would be safer to look someplace else for a meal. But the teeth aren't real—they are just part of the pattern on the bug's head.

Some predators use a disguise to help them catch their prey. The Sargassum Fish, for example, looks just like a piece of seaweed. When this fish hides in a clump of seaweed, other fish may not see it. They swim too close —and the Sargassum Fish snaps them up.

Big feet help a Jacana to get food. The feet spread the weight of the bird in such a way that the Jacana can walk on floating lily pads without falling into the water. It can walk to the center of a pond and feed on water bugs and small fish, and barely get its feet wet.

e may think that the huge nose of male Proboscis (pro-BOS-kiss) onkey is strange-looking. But fe- le Proboscis Monkeys find it ry attractive. A male with a large se is more likely to find a mate.

There are even animals that look like plants. The "flowers" below, for instance, are really Tube Worms that live in the ocean. The beautiful plumes are used by the worms to gather small bits of food from the water and carry the food to their mouths.

Sometimes, animals keep themselves safe by look- ing dead. The shell of the Venus Comb looks like the picked-over bones of a dead fish. Predators often stay away from the shell because they assume that there is no food to be found there.

Moving around is something that most animals must do on a regular basis. An animal must move to find food, or to find a mate, or to escape from trouble, or to find a place where it will have a better chance of surviving. Many animals perform fantastic feats when they move. They may move very fast, or very far, or their movements may take them into places where they don't seem to belong.

Sooty Terns can fly without stopping for five years! At the rate of 150 movements of the wings per minute, this means a Sooty Tern may flap its wings *400 million times* before finally landing. The birds eat on the wing and sleep on the wing, and only land when it is time for them to mate.

Most fish are content to stay in the water, but the Mudskipper likes to climb trees. It has a sucker on the underside of its body that helps it to hold on, and it uses its front flippers to push itself along. It has special gills that allow it to take oxygen directly from the air.

Squid use a kind of jet power to fly through the air. When a squid is swimming in the water, it uses a jet of water to push itself along. Water is squirted at great pressure out of a nozzle on the squid's body (see picture). At times, the squid can swim so fast that it may pop out of the water and glide through the air for long distances.

Under the ground, nothing moves as fast as a Star-nosed Mole. In soft soil, this furry little animal can dig a tunnel 150 feet long (46 meters) in less than an hour. It uses the star-shaped feelers on its nose to test the ground ahead of it, finding out where the soil is easiest to dig. The sharp claws move at great speed, like 10 small shovels. The energy that the mole uses is incredible. To keep itself going, it must eat its own weight in food every 24 hours.

The Sea Robin can swim and walk. It has spines on either side of its body that act like legs, holding it up as it moves along the bottom of the ocean. The spines are also used as feelers, to probe in the sand for food.

A squid may fly for 100 feet or more before it splashes back into the water.

The slowest mammal on earth is the Tree Sloth (SLOW-th). It hangs upside down in trees and usually moves at a speed of only 6 feet (2 meters) per minute. When it is really excited, it can reach a speed of 14 feet (4 meters) per minute. To get an idea of how slow a sloth is, why don't *you* try to walk only 6 feet in one minute?

The Colugo of Malaysia has a living parachute. A large membrane of skin attached to its body catches the air and holds the animal up just like a parachute. Using the membrane, the Colugo can float through the air for 100 yards (91 meters) or more.

9

Birds like to eat caterpillars. Some caterpillars are protected from birds because they look bad to eat or like dangerous animals. This caterpillar looks like a snake, and this scares birds away. Did you think this was a snake?

Getting food is a very important part of every animal's life. Some active animals spend most of the time when they are awake looking for food, catching it, or eating it. Others, like some reptiles, can live for a long time on a single meal. Some animals chase their prey, and others may trap it. In general, the amount of time, energy, and ingenuity that animals put into getting food can be truly incredible.

Honeypot Ants have a strange way of storing food. The ants live in the desert, where food is only available for part of the year. To survive, they store food—using members of the ant colony as living storage jars. The ants are stuffed with food and hung from the ceiling in special storage rooms within the ant nest.

Some animals use tools to get their food. Sea Otters are often seen using stones to crack open the hard shells of crabs and sea urchins.

A few animals use parts of their bodies as tools for getting food. The Aye Aye (EYE-eye) of Madagascar has an extra-long finger on each of its hands that it uses for prying bugs out of small holes in the bark of trees. It also uses the fingers to get the yolk out of eggs. The Aye Aye bites a hole in the end of an egg and dips a finger into the hole. Then it sucks the yolk off the finger.

Some insects build clever traps to catch their food. The Ant Lion builds a funnel of sand to trap ants. The more the ant struggles to escape, the more the sand crumbles under its feet. The ant slides down and down—and the Ant Lion catches it.

The Water Spider builds a unique air chamber under water to help it catch its food. Like all spiders, it must breathe air or it will drown. So it spins a very tight web of silk that is flat on top. Then it brings bubbles of air down from above and traps them under the web. The spider is then ready to sit in its underwater house and wait for food to swim by.

It's hard to believe, but some frogs really do jump out of the water and catch flying birds. A big Bullfrog can be 8 inches long (20 centimeters), and they can jump very fast. The frog sits in the water with only its eyes showing. And when a small bird flies over the water, the frog makes a tremendous leap.

Robber Crabs climb trees to find their food. Often, they will climb more than 50 feet (15 meters) up the trunks of palm trees to get young coconuts to eat. Once they reach the top, they cut off the coconuts with their gigantic pincers. The pincers are so strong that they can bend a piece of metal.

13

Chameleons have tongues that are longer than their bodies. The tongues are sticky on the end, for catching insects. A special set of muscles in the mouth of the chameleon can shoot the tongue out at incredible speed. When the tongue is not being used, it is bunched up in the mouth, like a pushed-up sleeve.

Staying alive is obviously *the* most important thing that all animals must do. To stay alive, they must get enough to eat — and make sure at the same time that other animals don't eat them. For this purpose, some animals have structures and ways of behaving that are truly incredible.

Almost every animal on earth has some way of defending itself. Some animals are fast. They defend themselves by running away. If they can outrun their predators, they will stay safe. Many animals are not fast enough to get away, so they hide themselves and hope that predators won't see them.

Most birds and many insects simply fly away from trouble. And they live in trees where fewer predators can get at them. Some harmless animals (such as the Alligator Bug shown earlier in this book) try to *look* dangerous to scare predators away.

There are animals that have weapons, such as claws and teeth, that they can use to defend themselves. And there are others that have shells (like turtles) or sharp spines (like porcupines) to keep their enemies from getting too close.

At times, animals must defend themselves from larger things than predators. Natural disasters, such as floods and droughts, can threaten animals more than predators do. Some animals (such as the ants below) have found ways to survive disasters.

When some animals are threatened, they roll up into a tight ball. The armor of a Three-banded Armadillo (shown at left) covers it up completely when it rolls into a ball. And the sharp spines of the Hedgehog (shown above) stick out in all directions when it gets all balled up.

The shapes and colors of many insects make it almost impossible to see them if they don't move. A wonderful example of this is the Wandering Leaf Insect of Malaysia. You really have to look hard to tell what part of the picture below is leaf and what part is insect.

In tropical parts of the world, heavy rains often cause floods. To keep from drowning when the water rises, some types of ants join their bodies together to form a kind of boat. As this "boat" floats along, it rolls over and over. So all of the ants spend some time under water and some time above water, where they can breathe.

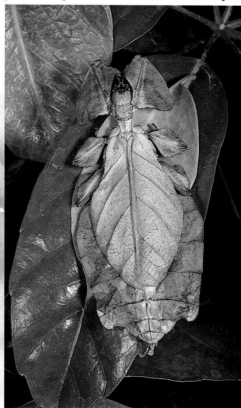

A hungry predator may think that it has captured a meal when it grabs a Gecko Lizard by the tail. But the predator is usually mistaken—because geckos can separate themselves from their tails whenever they want. By using special muscles, a gecko just pops its tail off and keeps running. Later on, it can grow a new tail to replace the one it has lost.

The Bombardier Beetle makes things hot for ants and other insects that attack it. Inside its body, the beetle has a special chamber in which it can mix two chemicals together. When the two chemicals are mixed, they react violently to each other and start to boil. The red-hot mixture is then sprayed all over the beetle's enemies.

17

Pentatomid bugs hatching.

Building is one of the most astonishing things that animals can do. We humans are in the habit of thinking that only we can build houses and bridges and places to store food. But animals build all of these things — and in most cases, they were building them a long time before people ever thought about building them. It may even be that people first learned to build certain things by watching animals.

The nest of a Potter Wasp is made of mud and looks like a small clay pot. Before the wasp lays an egg in the nest, it stings some small caterpillars and puts them in (as shown in the picture). This will give the wasp that hatches from the egg something to feed on as it grows inside the pot.

Green leaves are used by Tailor Ants to make their nests. To begin the job, a group of ants pulls two leaves together until their edges are touching (as shown above). Then the ants use fine silk strings to bind the leaves together.

The other end of the tunnel has a high lip. Air flowing over this lip creates a partial vacuum and draws air out of the tunnel.

One end of the tunnel has a low lip, to make it easy for air to enter.

Prairie Dogs had systems for circulating air in their homes for thousands of years before people ever thought of it. The Prairie Dogs build their burrows in such a way that fresh air is constantly flowing through the tunnels.

To make its nest, the Weaverbird actually weaves grass into a kind of basket. It uses the same basic techniques that people use in making baskets and weaving. Do you suppose that ancient people may have learned how to make baskets by watching weaverbirds?

A female Sand Wasp uses a kind of hammer to help her when she builds her nest. After digging a small hole in the ground, she lays an egg in it. Then she fills in the hole with loose sand. To pack the sand down, she picks up a pebble and taps the ground with it. These wasps are the only insects that are known to use tools of any kind.

A male Bower Bird puts together a wonderful display of colorful objects to attract a female. The display may contain such things as snail shells, bits of ribbon, flowers, and pieces of colored glass. And everything in it is usually the same color. The bird keeps arranging and adding to the display until he is successful in attracting a mate.

Army Ants use their own bodies to build bridges. When a group of them reaches a place that it cannot cross, some of the ants link their legs together, and the others walk over them.

Some tropical termites build mounds with overhanging roofs. The roofs help to keep heavy rains from damaging the walls of the mounds. Most of the water slides off the edges of the roofs and doesn't even touch the walls.

21

Animal Wonders are everywhere in this wonderful world. In this book, we have been showing you some of the most spectacularly unusual animals in the world. But when you think about it, *every* animal on earth is a wonder...including many animals that we see every day and take for granted.

When you really look at the animals around you, you will quickly discover that they all have something that is interesting or beautiful about them. Look at a dog or a cat, at a bird or a fly, at a snail or a rabbit. They all have unique ways of getting food, having babies, moving around, and defending themselves. They are all animal wonders.

Bees dance to let other bees know where to find food. When one bee finds food, it returns to the hive and "describes" the location of the food by the way it moves its body. This method is so precise that a bee can tell the others how much food there is, what direction they must fly, and how far they must go.

King Penguins have very odd nests—they carry their eggs around on their *feet*. When female penguins lay their eggs, the males pick them up and balance them on their feet until the eggs hatch. After the young are born, both the mother and the father may take turns carrying them on their feet. Emperor Penguins are the only other penguins that do this.

Sea Turtles cry salty tears as they crawl up on the beach to lay their eggs. But it isn't because they are sad. Instead, they are simply releasing extra salt from their bodies through glands near their eyes. They drink salt water while swimming at sea, and must get rid of the extra salt that this puts into their blood.

Three kinds of land frogs can be frozen as solid as an ice cube—*and still stay alive*. They spend the winter frozen completely stiff, but when the spring comes they thaw out and hop away.

The "mother" of a Seahorse is its father. When a female seahorse lays eggs, she puts them into a special pouch on the body of the male. And the male carries the eggs until little seahorses hatch out of them.

When migrating, Spiny Lobsters play a strange game of "follow the leader." Thousands of them hook themselves together into a long line, and then march along in single file for many miles.

Jumping Spiders can jump for incredible distances—up to *40 times* the length of their own bodies. The big eyes in front of the spider's head help it to judge how far it must jump to catch its prey.

Index